Invoking the Archangels Workbook

A Nine-Step Process to Heal Your Body, Mind and Soul

By Sunny Dawn Johnston

Sunny Dawn Johnston Productions

Copyright © 2014

ISBN-13: 978-0692249796

ISBN-10: 0692249796

Contents

Step 1 - "Awareness"
Step 2 - "Look Within"
Step 3 - "Choice"
Step 4 - "Commitment"
Step 5 - "Responsibility"
Step 6 - "Action"
Step 7 - "Release and replenish"
Step 8 - "Maintenance"
Step 9 - "Appreciation"

Introduction

In writing the book, **_Invoking the Archangels - A Nine-Step Process to Heal Your Body, Mind and Soul,_** I discovered the power of the written word. I have journaled, on and off, throughout my life. However, writing a book was a completely different experience for me. Even more so, I found that seeing your experience in black and white, in bold writing in front of you, has a lot more power than I was aware of. Within days of completing the manuscript for the book, I felt a stirring within to create a workbook to support you, the reader. It is my intention that this workbook be a sort of "best friend" to support you through the 9 step process of Healing your mind, body and soul. Throughout each section of this workbook, there are experiential exercises. I offer them to you as a way of truly connecting with yourself, your angels and your spirit. I suggest that you take the time to do each of ne the exercises fully and completely, for the very best possible results. If there is writing involved, please, take the time to do it, and don't skip over it. There is more value in doing the work than I can explain here. Once you have committed to doing the exercises in this workbook, you took will understand the importance of it.
~ Enjoy the journey to healing

~ Sunny

Developing Your Personal Relationship with Each Archangel

In my experience, this process has allowed me to connect to the energy of each Archangel and to allow healing to occur on many levels. It is important to me that you have your own experience with each Archangel so I have created an exercise to assist you in developing that relationship. I recommend you do this FIRST, before you read anything about the Archangels, or learn any more than you already know. This is an experiential exercise based on YOUR intuitive guidance. The worksheet lists each day of the week in a column down the left hand side of the page, I'd like you to write down one of the following colors next to each day of the week: blue, pink, yellow, green, white, red, and violet. Let your intuition guide you and ask your Angels for assistance. Once you have the seven colors matched up to each day of the week, you can continue reading.

Monday _blue_

Tuesday _pink_

Wednesday _yellow_

Thursday _green_

Friday _white_

Saturday _red_

Sunday _violet_

The Archangels and
Your Personal Experience

1. Archangel Michael:

Means "He who is like God"

Michael is the Archangel of protection,

guidance and strength.

Helps with: Protection, direction, self-esteem, motivation, courage, commitment, faith, energy, vitality, life's purpose, and releasing fear.

Color Vibration: Brilliant Blue

Gemstone: Lapis Lazuli

Invocation: I invoke the blue light of Archangel Michael to surround me and protect me from any negative energy or entities seen or unseen. I ask that I be a channel of divine love and healing to everyone I cross paths with. I ask for courage, strength and faith so that I may walk this earth with an open heart and an open mind. Thank you for the true and perfect guidance that surrounds me each and every moment … and so it is!

Visualization: As I invoke Archangel Michael, I visualize a sapphire blue bubble – like an energy field completely surrounding me. I imagine myself completely embraced by this beautiful brilliant energy, and as I do, I know that I am completely surrounded and protected from any negative energy.

Personal Experience:

_____

_____

_____

_____

_____

_____

_____

_____

_____

_____

_____

_____

_____

_____

_____

_____

2. Archangel Jophiel:

Means "Beauty of God"

Jophiel is the Archangel of creativity,

beauty and art.

Helps with: Manifesting more beauty in our lives through our thoughts, supports artists and artistic projects, release prejudice and ignorance, interior design and decorating, awakening, self-awareness, inspiration, hope and joy. Helps those who feel spiritually lost, depressed, or in despair.

Color Vibration: Golden Yellow

Gemstone: Citrine

Invocation: I invoke the golden yellow light of Archangel Jophiel. Help me to manifest beauty within and around me. Jophiel, I know that I am a creative being and I ask that you help me to use that creative power in every aspect of my life. Please help me to remember that whatever I focus on is manifested through the vibration of my own thoughts. Help me to align my thoughts with who I really am and to see the beauty in all that crosses my path. I will remain open-minded and be guided by the light within. With your help and creative power, I can and will manifest the beautiful life of my dreams … and so it is!

Visualization: As I invoke Archangel Jophiel, I visualize a golden yellow light entering the top of my head and moving down my entire body. This vibrating light encases me in a safe and comfortable energy field. I see, hear, feel and know that the energy of creativity and manifestation surrounds me and dwells within me, at all times.

Personal Experience:

_____

_____

_____

_____

_____

_____

_____

_____

_____

_____

_____

_____

_____

_____

_____

_____

_____

_____

_____

_____

_____

_____

_____

_____

3. Archangel Chamuel:

Means "He who sees or seeks God"

Chamuel is the Archangel of unconditional love

and adoration.

Helps with: Career, life purpose, finding lost items, building and strengthening relationships, world peace, and seeking soul mates.

Color Vibration: Pink

Gemstone: Rose Quartz, Rhodochrosite, Pink Rhodonite

Invocation: I invoke the unconditional love and light of Archangel Chamuel. Please heal any and all emotional wounds or pain that holds me back from truly loving myself as the divine Spirit that I am. Archangel Chamuel, please help me to open my heart to the beauty within me as well as around me. Allow me to see myself through your angelic vibration and feel love as I release any and all resentments, fears and pain. I ask to experience forgiveness, self-acceptance and unconditional self love. Thank you for helping me attract positive, kind, gentle, and non-judgmental love into myself and my life … and so it is!

Visualization: As I invoke Archangel Chamuel, I imagine a vibrant pink energy surrounding my entire physical being. As I breathe in, I see that pink energy moving into my heart and filling me with unconditional love and the gentle energy of Archangel Chamuel.

Personal Experience:

_____

_____

_____

_____

_____

_____

_____

_____

_____

_____

_____

_____

_____

_____

_____

_____

_____

_____

_____

_____

_____

_____

_____

_____

_____

_____

_____
_____
_____
_____
_____
_____
_____
_____
_____
_____
_____
_____
_____
_____
_____
_____
_____
_____
_____
_____
_____
_____
_____
_____
_____
_____
_____
_____

4. Archangel Gabriel:

Means "God is my strength"

Gabriel is the Archangel of communication.

Helps with: Communication in any area, TV and radio work, adoption, child conception and fertility, journalism and writing.

Color Vibration: White

Gemstone: Moonstone, clear quartz

Invocation: I now invoke the mighty and powerful Archangel Gabriel and his energy of communication and strength. Please bring me insight and awareness so that I may always speak my truth. Remove all doubts and fears, and allow me to express myself in a loving way through mind, body and Spirit. Please help me to share my words in a way that is gentle, kind and loving. Please help me to communicate from my heart. Thank you and so it is."

Visualization: As I invoke Archangel Gabriel's energy I visualize the white light of Gabriel coming down from the heavens and entering my body through my head. As I sit in this energy, I feel clarity about communication in my throat area, and I say thank you, out loud, to allow that clear communication to move completely through me.

Personal Experience:

_____

_____

_____

_____

_____

_____

_____

_____

_____

_____

_____

_____

_____

_____

_____

_____

_____

_____

_____

_____

_____

_____

_____

_____

_____

_____

_____

_____

5. Archangel Raphael:

Means "God heals or God has healed"

Archangel Raphael is the angel of healing.

Helps with: Eliminating or reducing addictions and cravings, healing on all levels, guidance and support for healers, physical and spiritual eyesight, clairvoyance, and finding lost pets.

Color Vibration: Green

Gemstone: Jade or Aventurine

Invocation: I ask Archangel Raphael to surround me in his healing vibration of emerald green light. I am in need of healing at this time and I ask that you infuse me with your healing energy. Please surround me and fill me with health, well-being and wholeness. Help me to heal any wounds - physically, mentally, emotionally and spiritually - from the past or present. Heal and restore every aspect of my being for the highest good of all ... and so it is!

Visualization: As I invoke Archangel Raphael's energy, I see the emerald green energy completely surround my body. I feel this energy moving within me and I affirm that I am healthy and whole and that well-being is my divine birthright.

Personal Experience:

_____

_____

_____

_____

_____

_____

_____

_____

_____

_____

_____

_____

_____

_____

_____

_____

_____

_____

_____

_____

_____

_____

_____

_____

_____

_____

_____

6. Archangel Uriel:

Means "God is Light or God's Light"

Uriel is the Archangel that offers illumination

and transmutation.

Helps with: Insight, clarity, peace, vision, problem-solving, writing, new ideas, study, tests, and students.

Color Vibration: Purple/Gold seen usually as Ruby Red

Gemstone: Amber, Ruby

Invocation: I invoke the wise and peaceful energy of Archangel Uriel to completely surround my physical and energetic body. Please help soothe all conflict in my life and replace it with peace, clarity and insight. I ask you to help me release any mental or emotional patterns that keep me stuck in my fears. I ask that you fill me with the knowingness of who I really am. Please help me to trust my experiences, so I may see the greater vision, understand the value of each and grow in a way that serves all. I am blessed to be on this journey of life and I thank you Uriel for your continued guidance, wisdom and vision … and so it is!

Visualization: As I invoke Archangel Uriel's energy of Wisdom, I imagine or visualize myself completely enveloped in the color red. I take a deep breath in and see, hear, feel and know that Archangel Uriel is guiding me throughout my physical journey.

Personal Experience:

_____

_____

_____

_____

_____

_____

_____

_____

_____

_____

_____

_____

_____

_____

_____

_____

_____

_____

_____

_____

_____

_____

_____

_____

_____

7. Archangel Zadkiel:

Means "Righteousness of God"

Zadkiel is the Archangel of forgiveness, mercy, and benevolence.

Helps with: Forgiveness of self and others, emotional healing, compassion, freedom, finding lost objects, and memory.

Color Vibration: Violet

Gemstone: Amethyst

Invocation: I invoke the energy of Archangel Zadkiel. I ask you to surround me in your light of forgiveness and mercy. Please help me soften my heart so that I may forgive myself and help support me in releasing my pain, bitterness, and negativity. Help me remove any and all obstacles that stand in the way of my connection to the deeper love I know I have within me ... and so it is!

Visualization: As I invoke Archangel Zadkiel, I visualize a violet flame just above my head. I imagine this flame absorbing all of the negative thoughts, feelings and emotions that hold me back from forgiving myself and others. I allow all of the lower vibrational energies to be absorbed by Zadkiel's loving violet energy.

Personal Experience:

_____

_____

_____

_____

_____

_____

_____

_____

_____

_____

_____

_____

_____

_____

_____

_____

_____

_____

_____

_____

_____

_____

_____

Experiential Exercises

with each of the Archangels

Doing each of these exercises daily, will help you to develop a stronger relationship, not only with the Archangels, but also with yourself. I suggest after taking the first week to do the exercise on page 2 to connect with each Archangel, that you do each of these exercises every day, for 21 days. It is best to keep notes about any experiences throughout the entire 21 days. This will help you begin to see much more clearly how exactly the angels are manifesting in your life. Just take a few minutes each day to do each one of these exercises. At most it may take an hour; but, think of what you could gain. All I am asking for is 21 days. After that, you will know the Archangels, their vibrations and most importantly, you will see and feel their presence in your life, daily! ~ Enjoy these exercises - I do!

~ Sunny

1. Archangel Michael – Blue Bubble – Prayer of Protection

To experience Michael's energy, it is important to learn to protect and maintain your own energy. For the next 21 days, every morning before you get out of bed, I'd like you to use the Prayer of Protection that is in the Appendix of the book ***Invoking the Archangels - A Nine-Step Process to Heal Your Body, Mind and Soul,***. Take time to ground your energy, and connect with Mother Earth and your physical body through your feet; then connect with the white light energy of Spirit through your crown. Finally, step into the vibration of Archangel Michael by visualizing a giant energy field, almost a bubble-type of energy in front of you. Once you can see, feel or know that this blue vibrating energy is just before you, I'd like you to imagine stepping into it, so that it completely surrounds your entire physical body. As you allow this to happen, take a deep breath in, and simply know that you are now protected by the energy of Archangel Michael.

Personal Experience:

_____

_____

_____

_____

_____

_____

2. Archangel Jophiel – Mirror Mirror – Seeing Your Own Beauty

The exercise I would like for you to do to truly bring in Archangel Jophiel's energy, is the Mirror exercise. Every day, at least 3 times a day, I'd like you to go and stand/sit in front of a mirror. As you look into your soul, through your eyes (not at the lines or dimples or acne) I'd like you to say to yourself, "I am worthy, I am deserving, I am loving, I am receiving, I am perfect, I am whole, I am amazing." Continue affirming as many more positive affirmations as you can until at least 5 minutes have gone by. It is important to maintain eye contact with yourself throughout the exercise. This may be hard … that is ok. If you will do it, this will be one of the most important exercises you can do to allow yourself to see your own beauty. Remember: 3 times a day, for at least 5 minutes each!

Personal Experience:

_____

_____

_____

_____

_____

_____

_____

3. Archangel Chamuel – I ♥ Me – Affirmation (Say, Write, Feel, Repeat)

To experience Archangel Chamuel's loving energy I suggest you begin to affirm what it is you want to experience in your life, how you want to feel, what you want to see. So, we will begin with these affirmations. Each day, I'd like you to say each affirmation aloud, and then write the affirmation down, and bring in the feeling of the affirmation. When bringing in the feeling, sometimes people will say, "well, I haven't felt that in a long time." It doesn't matter when you felt it last - just go to a time when you did, and take a breath to breathe it in. For example: if your affirmation is "I am Peace", go to a time in your life when you felt peace. It could have been when you were 5 years old, it doesn't matter when, just bring the feeling in, take a deep breath allowing that energy to move through you, and then release.

Do each one of these affirmation exercises 3 times:

Say, write, feel, repeat … Say, write, feel, repeat … Say, write, feel, repeat.

I am loved, unconditionally

_____

_____

_____

I am open to love

_____

_____

_____

I am willing to receive

_____

_____

_____

I trust

_____

_____

_____

I am open to healing my heart

_____

_____

_____

I am thankful for my life

_____

_____

_____

I see my beauty

_____

_____

_____

I am worthy, simply because I am

_____

_____

_____

The Universe is supporting me, always

_____

_____

_____

I accept love

_____

_____

_____

I am healthy, whole and complete

_____

_____

_____

My inner voice and feelings guide me

_____

_____

_____

I know that I am all I need to be

_____

_____

_____

I accept the angels' love

_____

_____

_____

I am light

_____

_____

_____

I can do anything I truly desire

_____

_____

_____

I am divinely guided

_____

_____

_____

I live, laugh and love often

_____

_____

_____

I am peace

_____

_____

_____

I am positive

_____

_____

_____

I trust myself and my choices

_____

_____

_____

I believe in me

_____

_____

_____

4. Archangel Gabriel – Scribe Messages From Above – Automatic Writing

To connect with Archangel Gabriel's energy we will do automatic writing. There are several ways to receive messages in this way. The easiest is to begin by saying a prayer, asking Gabriel to surround you and guide you. Once you have called him in, I want you to think about a question you have in your life right now. Just take a minute or two to focus your energy on the question. Once you have done this, write the question here in this section. After that, ask for the answer to come to you and through you. Now begin writing - anything and everything that comes to you. Just allow yourself to let go and just write. The message may come in sentences, poems, single words, or complete stories. You could also feel as if it is random thoughts. Either way, just continue to write, for at least 5 minutes. If you can write longer, and are enjoying the process, please do. The important part in this exercise is to not stop writing; you want your hand to be moving, even if you don't have anything coming. If you are stuck, simply write "Archangel Gabriel come to me" over and over and over. It is common when beginning this exercise to have pages of those requests. However, the more you can let go of the thoughts in your head, go with the flow, and let the energy move you, you will begin to get messages. Sometimes, it will feel like you are just writing what is in your head; and in the beginning that may, in fact, be the case. But, if you continue to do this exercise every day for 3 weeks, you will see a difference - not only in the messages, but in the writing. You will notice a difference in the messages that come from your head versus the ones that come from the Angels. This is a great way to connect, and once you get comfortable with it, it will be a wonderful tool for you to receive answers as well as to help others.

Personal Experience:

_____

_____

_____

_____

_____

_____

_____

_____

_____

_____

_____

_____

_____

_____

_____

_____

_____

_____

_____

_____

5. Archangel Raphael – Feel Your Heartbeat – Healing Energy

To experience Archangel Raphael's healing energy, we begin by putting your hands on your heart. As you allow your breath to move naturally through your body, just become an observer of your breath. Don't try to make it anything different than it is. After observing your breath for a few minutes, I'd like you to then visualize as you breathe. When you breathe in, you breathe in the loving energy or Archangel Raphael. See, hear, feel and know that the beautiful emerald green energy you are breathing in is healing you, mind, body and soul. See it enter in through your nose and feel the healing energy move through your entire body. Now on the exhale, hear the breath as it is released from your body and know that you have begun to allow the healing to occur. Another way to experience Raphael's energy is to focus on your breath, and as you breathe in, you breathe in love, life, healing joy, energy, passion, etc. And as you breathe out, you release and let go of pain, sadness, frustration, anger, fear, guilt, etc. After 15 minutes, I'd like you to journal your awareness of your experience. Just jot down anything that you became aware of. I suggest you do this exercise every night, before you go to bed, for 3 straight weeks to really connect with Archangel Raphael's energy of healing.

Personal Experience:

6. Archangel Uriel – I See Me – Visualize & See the Bigger Picture

To connect with Archangel Uriel's energy, think of a situation that is challenging to you. This could be an experience that is either past or current. I'd like you to take a few moments and think about that experience. Write down, very briefly, a sentence or two about the situation. Once you have done this, I would like you to meditate for 5 minutes with the intention of seeing the greater vision, the bigger picture or the purpose. You may come away from the meditation with a sense or a feeling, words or sentences, images or symbols, or a complete knowing of how to shift your energy and focus in a positive way to transmute the challenge and raise the vibration to a higher state. The first time you may not have any awareness at all. But I would like you to do this once a day, 3 days in a row with the same challenge. Your intention is to gain clarity and a positive perspective on your challenge. Once you have done this exercise for 3 days, you can move on to a new challenge.

Personal Experience:

_____

_____

_____

_____

_____

7. Archangel Zadkiel – I Take My Power Back – Forgiveness

To experience the powerful energy of Archangel Zadkiel, I suggest you begin to take your power back. Remember, no one can take your power away without your permission; so even if unknowingly, you give your power away. In this exercise, think of a particular person that you have given your power away to. So let's say it is a person named Erik. I'd like you to imagine that both of you are connected by a cord, with a plug on each end. In this visualization, imagine that you unplug from Erik by seeing yourself pull the plug out of him, essentially taking your power back. Next, it is essential you send him love. You can visualize the color pink filling up the area that you were plugged into; or ask Archangel Chamuel to surround him and support him. Once you have done this, the next step is for you to quickly visualize yourself unplugging as well. If you don't do this step, you will end up plugging into someone else that vibrates at the same level as the person you just unplugged from. Now that you have unplugged yourself, fill yourself up the same way you filled Erik – with the color pink and unconditional love. It is important that you do this every morning and every night for the next 3 weeks. You will begin to feel stronger, more alive, and you will know that this "I take my power back" exercise is empowering you and filling you up. You may choose different people each time, or the same, based on your situation, need and experience. At least once a day, journal what you felt or became aware of as you were doing this exercise.

Personal Experience:

The 9 Step Archangel Process
to Healing Your Heart

This is an opportunity for you to use this 9-step process on any issue or challenge, past or present, that you are not feeling in appreciation of. Take some deep breaths, focus on your heart space, invite the Archangels to surround you, and then focus on a particular issue or challenge that you want to release, forgive, heal, see a new perspective of and find appreciation for. By using these steps you can walk yourself from awareness to appreciation. If it is a current experience, you might find that you can't move immediately from where you are at this time, which is ok. Walk through the steps you have already experienced, look forward to the steps that lay ahead, invoke the Archangels, and you will begin to move, from this moment forward, toward appreciation.

In this section of the workbook, I not only ask you to think about and feel each step and your experience as you move through them , but also, to write down your experiences, one by one. So begin with an issue, a challenge, either past or present and go through all of the steps. Once you have found appreciation in that experience, you can then move to the next one. If this is a past experience, walking yourself through each step, from where you stand today, can change your perspective of the "issue" and move you to a place of appreciation - which is also a place of forgiveness. For a current challenge, just begin with Step One. There is no right or wrong amount of time. Just take the first step, and have the willingness to move forward. The answers are already within you, the appreciation is already there, you are just on an inward journey to find it. Let's start steppin'!

I believe you too will see and feel the power of the written word. When you write your story, the emotions begin to come up differently than in telling it. When you see your story on paper, it brings up those emotions that can then be released. The emotions this exercise can bring up and out are profound, especially if you are feeling resistance to it. Resistance tells me the power of it is undeniable ... as is the love that you have around you, the Archangels surrounding you, and the healing you have within you! Enjoy the journey!

Feel free to make as many copies as you need of these following pages so that you can work the steps. There is power in working them through written form and not just in your head.

Issue/Challenge

STEP 1 - Awareness

Awareness is the state or ability to perceive, to feel, or to be conscious of. Typically you become aware of a challenge, an illness, an emotion, or a desire. You can also have self-awareness. Self-awareness is the ability to perceive one's own existence, traits, feelings and behaviors. You become aware of your own personality or individuality.

Personal Experience:

_____

_____

_____

_____

_____

_____

_____

_____

_____

_____

_____

STEP 2 - Look within

You have to have a willingness to look within and ask for help. Unfortunately, many of us look outside of ourselves for answers to our questions. The key is to get in touch with the inner you, and acknowledge the intuitive power that you have. Oftentimes decisions are based from the ego and not the spirit. By looking within, the path becomes clear and uncluttered.

Personal Experience:

_____

_____

_____

_____

_____

_____

_____

_____

_____

_____

_____

_____

_____

_____

_____

_____

STEP 3 - Choice

Choice simply means the act of choosing. You always have a choice to act or react. The kind of life you have is the life you choose. In this process, choice is the foundation of change. Sometimes you perceive your choice as a right choice or a wrong choice; but my point is – you still have a choice.

Personal Experience:

_____

_____

_____

_____

_____

_____

_____

_____

_____

_____

_____

_____

_____

_____

_____

STEP 4 - Commitment

The most important single factor in an individual's success is commitment. Commitment ignites action. To commit means to devote yourself to a purpose or cause.

Personal Experience:

_____

_____

_____

_____

_____

_____

_____

_____

_____

_____

_____

_____

_____

_____

_____

_____

_____

_____

_____

_____

_____

STEP 5 - Responsibility

Responsibility means accepting that you and you alone are accountable for your life. There is no one to blame. Being responsible comes with the realization that you are where you are because of your own conduct, beliefs, and behavior. Your choices have created the experiences you are living right now. The good news is that you are responsible for your life. The bad news is that you are responsible for your life.

Personal Experience:

_____

_____

_____

_____

_____

_____

_____

_____

_____

_____

_____

_____

_____

_____

_____

_____

STEP 6 - Action

Action is the state or process of acting or doing something in order to achieve a purpose. In this step, you take action and you invoke the healing energy of the Archangels.

Personal Experience:

_____

_____

_____

_____

_____

_____

_____

_____

_____

_____

_____

_____

_____

_____

_____

_____

_____

_____

_____

STEP 7 - Releasing and Replenishing

Releasing is often defined as an emotional purging. Our emotions, thoughts, and beliefs are contained in our bodies ... so learning to release these will help you achieve more peace, happiness and emotional well-being. Replenishing simply means to fill back up or make complete again. Emotional purging often leaves empty spaces within - and since nature abhors a vacuum, you must fill yourself back up.

Personal Experience:

_____

_____

_____

_____

_____

_____

_____

_____

_____

_____

_____

_____

_____

_____

_____

STEP 8 - Maintenance

In this case, maintenance means to maintain and protect your own energy and vibration. It is important to protect your energy. If you don't do this, you risk breaking down your own energy resources at all levels - physical, emotional, mental and spiritual.

Personal Experience:

_____

_____

_____

_____

_____

_____

_____

_____

_____

_____

_____

_____

_____

_____

_____

STEP 9 - Appreciation

Appreciation is knowing or understanding the value of an experience and is often expressed with feelings of gratitude. In this step, it specifically means to honor an experience with open arms and a healed heart. Oftentimes, once appreciation is experienced, forgiveness follows.

Personal Experience:

_____

_____

_____

_____

_____

_____

_____

_____

_____

_____

_____

_____

_____

_____

_____

_____

_____

_____

Angelic Positive Affirmations

I am loved, unconditionally

I am open to my Guardian Angels

I am protected and guided by my Angels

I trust that my Guide will attract only miracles in my life

I am open to my Healing Angels

I am thankful for my life and my Angel of Perception

I am now surrounded by Angels

The Angels shine the love of the Universe upon me and
through me

I accept love from the Angels

I call upon the Archangels to help and guide me

My inner voice and feelings are guidance from the Angels

I know that the Angels love me and are guiding me right now
I accept the Angels' love

My Angels and I enjoy new opportunities to give service to the
world

The Angel of Inspiration guides me to do anything I truly
desire

I am divinely guided by the Angel of Happiness

I am divinely guided by the Angels to guide me towards
optimal health

I am Peace

I am divinely guided by the Angel of Patience

I Trust my loved ones will be protected by the Angels

I believe in the Universe's messengers, the Angels

Positive Affirmations

Body, Self Love, Prosperity, Love, Health, Career, Addiction

Body Image Affirmations

1. I release my body to accept healing and health.

2. I am accepting health in my body.

3. I am releasing my DNA to heal my body and mind.

4. I am health.

5. I am attracting people and information that will help me live a healthy life.

6. I am open to releasing unhealthy thoughts.

7. My health is important to me.

8. I came to this earth equipped to be healthy and live in health.

9. I see myself healthy and whole.

10. I see myself living in health.

11. I am letting my body heal itself.

12. My body is healing my being.

13. I release my past and leave it behind.

14. I am open to releasing unhealthy people.

15. My DNA is programmed to be healthy.

16. Being healthy is easy.

17. Being healthy is fun.

18. I am open to releasing unhealthy behaviors.

19. I release my body to find its perfect weight, whatever that may be.

20. I release my body to find its perfect eating plan, whatever that may be.

21. I release my being to find its perfect healthy lifestyle, whatever that may be.

22. I am open to learning about healthy activities I would like to be part of.

23. My body is important to me and I am committed to taking care of it.

24. My health is a priority.

25. I release my being to find health gently and lovingly.

Self Love

1. I am filled with light, love and peace.

2. I treat myself with kindness and respect.

3. I give myself permission to shine.

4. I honor the best parts of myself and share them with others.

5. I am proud of all I have accomplished.

6. Today I give myself permission to be greater than my fears.

7. I am my own best friend and cheerleader.

8. I have many qualities, traits and talents that make me unique.

9. I am a valuable human being.

10. I love myself just the way I am.

11. I love and forgive myself for any past mistakes.

12. I look in the mirror and I love what I see.

13. I recognize my many strengths.

14. I am my own best friend.

15. I am a lot stronger and more powerful than I think.

16. I have unlimited potential.

17. All the power is within me; I can achieve anything I set my mind to.

18. I am abundant.

19. I know that to achieve anything, all I have to do is to just take one step at a time.

20. Every day, in every way I am becoming better and better.

21. I strive for excellence in everything I do.

22. Every day in every way I am discovering new creative abilities within me and they are becoming a second nature to me.

23. I am good enough.

25. I can achieve anything I set my mind to.

Prosperity

1. My bank balance is always healthy.

2. Abundance flows to me.

3. I prosper in everything I do.

4. I am unlimited in my financial achievements.

5. I accept affluence.

6. I deserve prosperity.

7. I am a money magnet.

8. Money comes to me easily and effortlessly.

9. I hold prosperous thoughts.

10. My wealth is increasing every day.

11. *I open to the flow of great abundance in all areas of my life.*

12. *I always have more than enough of everything I need.*

13. *Today I expand my awareness of the abundance all around me.*

14. *I allow the universe to bless me in surprising and joyful way.*

15. *My grateful heart attracts more of everything I desire.*

16. *Prosperity surrounds me, prosperity fills me, prosperity flows to me and through me.*

17. *I exude passion, purpose and prosperity.*

18. *I am always led to the people who need what I have to offer.*

19. *As my commitment to help others grows, so does my wealth.*

20. *I enjoy my prosperity and share it freely with the world.*

21. *My income is growing higher and higher NOW.*

22. *I AM passionate about building wealth.*

23. *All resistance to prosperity has dissolved in total grace.*

24. *I deserve to have financial abundance in my life NOW.*

25. *I AM successful because I know what I want and I ask for it.*

Love

1. *I attract lasting, happy relationships into my life.*

2. *I welcome love into my life with open arms.*

3. *I deserve love and accept it now.*

4. *Love comes to me easily and effortlessly.*

5. *I give and receive love easily and joyfully.*

6. *I am ready for a healthy, loving relationship.*

7. *All of my relationships are meaningful and fulfilling.*

8. *As I share my love with others the universe mirrors love back to me.*

9. *I am a love magnet to the right partner.*

10. *I trust the universe to know the type of partner who is perfect for me.*

11. *Today I release fear and open my heart to true love .*

12. *I am grateful for the people in my life.*

13. *I am the perfect partner for my perfect partner .*

14. *I deserve a loving, healthy relationship.*

15. *I deserve to be loved and I allow myself to be loved.*

16. *I am a radiant being filled with light and love.*

17. *I now express love to all those I meet.*

18. *I am a radiating center of divine love.*

19. *Divine love is working through me now.*

20. *I bathe in the unconditional love of my Creator.*

21. *Love radiates from me at all times.*

22. *Others love me easily and joyfully.*

23. *I express love freely.*

24. *As I give love, I am instantly supplied with more.*

25. *I attract loving, beautiful people into my life.*

Health

1. *I have balance in my life.*

2. *Every day my mind is filled with positive thoughts creating a beautiful life for me.*

3. *I am beautiful.*

4. *The Choice is within me.*

5. *I have the choice to change.*

6. *I always have choices.*

7. *I am committed to excellence in everything I do.*

8. *I am an excellent person.*

9. *I seek excellence.*

10. *I am healthy, and full of energy and vitality.*

11. I am healthy.

12. I have vitality.

13. I am healthy, happy and radiant.

14. I am committed to a healthy life.

15. I am committed to eating healthy.

16. My commitment to exercise is reality.

17. I am committed to releasing weight.

18. I am committed to walking every day.

19. I nourish my mind, body and soul with positive affirmations.

20. I accept health as my normal state.

21. I have control of my health and wellness.

22. I have abundant energy and vitality.

23. I fill the energy I need to do all the daily activities in my life.

24. I take care of my body and it cares of me.

25. I will enjoy good health today.

Career

1. I easily achieve my goals.

2. I have absolute faith in my success.

3. *Success in mine to be enjoyed.*

4. *I am successful in all that I do.*

5. *I have everything I need to succeed.*

6. *I am living my dream.*

7. *I am experiencing fantastic success.*

8. *Today I open my mind to the endless opportunities surrounding me.*

9. *I boldly act on great opportunities when I see them.*

10. *My intuition leads me to the most lucrative opportunities.*

11. *An opportunity is simply a possibility until I act on it.*

12. *Today I see each moment as a new opportunity to express my greatness.*

13. *I expand my awareness of the hidden potential in each experience.*

14. *Each decision I make creates new opportunities.*

15. *I have the courage to follow my dreams and goals with passion.*

16. *I will accomplish what I set out to do, because I can.*

17. *I have enough knowledge and resources.*

18. *My career has taken off like a rocket.*

19. *I AM an expert in my field and I receive the perfect pay for my expertise.*

20. My career rewards me with freedom and monetary abundance.

21. I AM passionate about my career and it reflects in monetary reward.

22. I AM promoted to the top of the career ladder with matching funds and matching benefits.

23. I AM the top salesperson in my field with clients lined up for miles.

24. My phone is ringing off the hook with additional clients.

25. My career is overflowing with success, so much that I have hired additional help.

Addiction

1. I am perfect just as I am.

2. Every life experience carries a lesson.

3. I am free.

4. I accept myself.

5. I am deserving of love.

6. I accept life's challenges as a way to grow.

7. I open myself to healing, I have the right to be treated with respect.

8. I allow myself the proper amount of food, sleep and enjoyment each day.

9. *I am sober.*

10. *I forgive myself.*

11. *I choose letting go.*

12. *I am free from negative substances, people and energy.*

13. *I am responsible for my own happiness.*

14. *I lovingly take back my power.*

15. *I give myself permission to change.*

16. *No person, place, or thing has any power over me. I am free.*

17. *I create a new life with new rules that totally support me.*

18. *The past is over. I choose to love and approve of myself in the now.*

19. *I easily and comfortably release that which I no longer need in life.*

20. *I am doing the best I can. I am wonderful. I am at peace.*

21. *I am willing to change and grow. I now create a safe, new future.*

22. *I refuse to limit myself. I am always willing to take the next step.*

23. *I choose to handle all my experiences with love, joy, and ease.*

24. *I have the courage to change.*

25. I move beyond past limitations into the freedom of the now.

About the Author

SUNNY DAWN JOHNSTON is an inspirational speaker, a compassionate spiritual teacher, an internationally acclaimed psychic medium and an author. She has been featured on numerous local and national television and radio shows including *Coast to Coast* with George Noory. In 2003, Sunny founded Sunlight Alliance LLC., a spiritual teaching and healing center in Glendale, Arizona. She also volunteers her time as a psychic investigator for the international organization *FIND ME*. This is a not-for-profit organization of Psychic, Investigative, and Canine Search & Rescue (SAR) volunteers working together to provide leads to law enforcement and families of missing persons and homicide.

Sunny lives in the sunshine of the Arizona desert with her husband Brett, sons Crew and Arizona and their two dogs, Pelé and Xena. To learn more about Sunny's work, watch videos and read articles, please go to: http://www.sunnydawnjohnston.com

To join in a fun and interactive Facebook page, please check out: http://www.facebook.com/SunnyDawnJohnstonFanPage

Other Creations by
Sunny Dawn Johnston

Invoking the Archangels – To Heal Mind, Body & Soul

Embracing The Body That Is - A Guide To Loving Yourself

Soul Transitions - A Mediums Guide to the Spirit World

Sunny Dawn Johnston Meditations

 Conversations with Sunny

 Prosperity Affirmation CD

 Positive Affirmations CD

 The Love Never Ends – Messages From The Other Side

For a complete list of products by Sunny, please visit:

www.SunnyDawnJohnston.com

Made in the USA
San Bernardino, CA
21 August 2014